EASY JAZZ FAVORITES

15 Selections For Young Jazz Ensembles

Contents

HAL•LEONARD®
CORPORATION
7777 W. BLUEMOUND RD. P.O. BOX 13819 MILWAUKEE, WI 53213

AIN'T MISBEHAVIN'

Words by ANDY RAZAF
Music by THOMAS WALLER and HARRY BROOKS
Arranged by BOB LOWDEN

Trumpet 1

ALL THE THINGS YOU ARE
(From VERY WARM FOR MAY)

Lyrics by OSCAR HAMMERSTEIN II
Music by JEROME KERN
Arranged by MICHAEL SWEENEY

Trumpet 1

TRUMPET 1

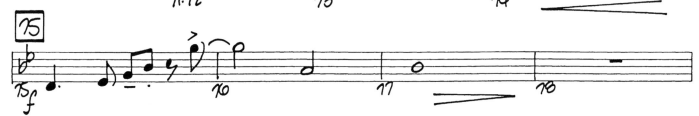

BLUE TRAIN
(Blue Trane)

TRUMPET 1

By JOHN COLTRANE
Arranged by MICHAEL SWEENEY

TRUMPET 1

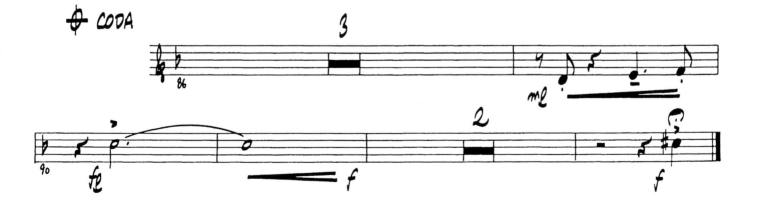

CARAVAN
(From SOPHISTICATED LADIES)

Words and Music by DUKE ELLINGTON
IRVING MILLS and JUAN TIZOL
Arranged by MICHAEL SWEENEY

Trumpet 1

TRUMPET 1

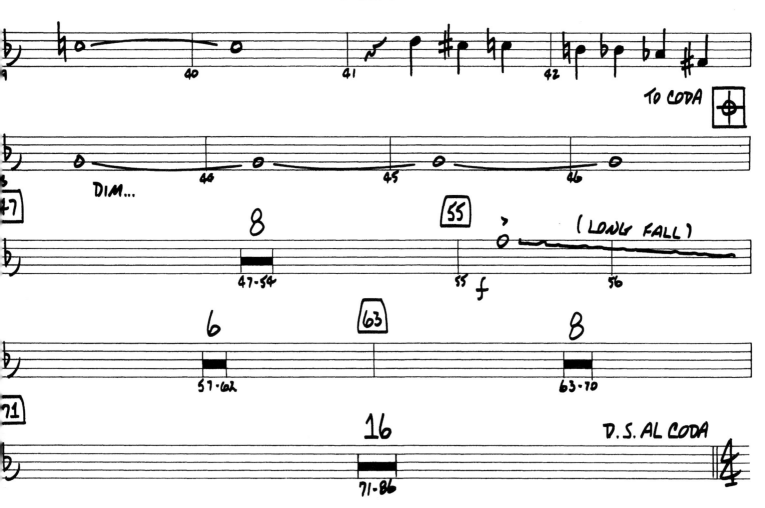

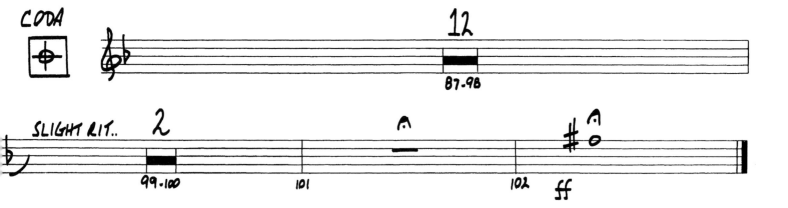

CHAMELEON

TRUMPET 1

By HERBIE HANCOCK, PAUL JACKSON,
HARVEY MASON and BENNIE MAUPIN
Arranged by MICHAEL SWEENEY

FLY ME TO THE MOON
(In Other Words)

TRUMPET 1

Words and Music by BART HOWARD
Arranged by JERRY NOWAK

TRUMPET 1

THE GIRL FROM IPANEMA
(Garôta De Ipanema)

TRUMPET 1

Original Words by VINICIUS DE MORAES
Music by ANTONIO CARLOS JOBIM
Arranged by JOHN BERRY

IN THE MOOD

TRUMPET 1

By JOE GARLAND
Arranged by MICHAEL SWEENEY

INSIDE OUT

By MICHAEL SWEENEY

TRUMPET 1

TRUMPET 1

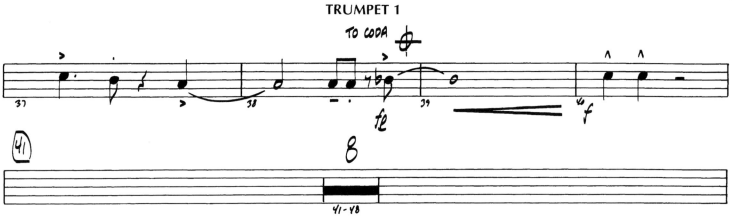

MILESTONES

TRUMPET 1

By MILES DAVIS
Arranged by PETER BLAIR

TRUMPET 1

A NIGHTINGALE SANG IN BERKELEY SQUARE

Lyric by ERIC MASCHWITZ
Music by MANNING SHERWIN
Arranged by ROGER HOLMES

Trumpet 1

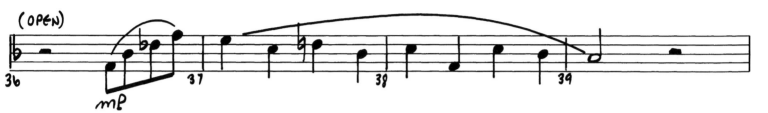

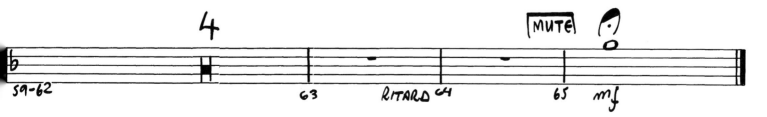

ONE NOTE SAMBA
(Samba De Uma Nota So)

Original Lyrics by NEWTON MENDONCA
English Lyrics by ANTONIO CARLOS JOBIM
Music by ANTONIO CARLOS JOBIM
Arranged by JERRY NOWAK

TRUMPET 1

MCA music publishing

TRUMPET 1

ROUTE 66

TRUMPET 1

By BOBBY TROUP
Arranged by MICHAEL SWEENEY

TRUMPET 1

ST. LOUIS BLUES

TRUMPET 1

Words and Music by W.C. HANDY
Arranged by MICHAEL SWEENEY

TRUMPET 1

WHEN I FALL IN LOVE

Words by EDWARD HEYMAN
Music by VICTOR YOUNG
Arranged by ROGER HOLMES

TRUMPET 1

TRUMPET 1